TOWN
CRIER

ABOUT THE LEXI RUDNITSKY FIRST BOOK PRIZE IN POETRY

The Lexi Rudnitsky First Book Prize in Poetry is a collaboration between Persea Books and The Lexi Rudnitsky Poetry Project. It sponsors the annual publication of a collection by a female-identifying poet who has yet to publish a full-length poetry book.

Lexi Rudnitsky (1972–2005) grew up outside of Boston. She studied at Brown University and Columbia University, where she wrote poetry and cultivated a profound relationship with a lineage of women poets that extends from Muriel Rukeyser to Heather McHugh. Her own poems exhibit both a playful love of language and a fierce conscience. Her writing appeared in *The Antioch Review*, *Columbia: A Journal of Literature and Art*, *The Nation*, *The New Yorker*, *The Paris Review*, *Pequod*, and *The Western Humanities Review*. In 2004, she won the Milton Kessler Memorial Prize for Poetry from *Harpur Palate*. Lexi died suddenly in 2005, just months after the birth of her first child and the acceptance for publication of her first book of poems, *A Doorless Knocking into Night* (Mid-List Press, 2006). The Lexi Rudnitsky First Book Prize in Poetry was founded to memorialize her and to promote the type of poet and poetry in which she so spiritedly believed.

Previous winners of the Lexi Rudnitsky First Book Prize in Poetry

2019 Sara Wainscott, *Insecurity System*
2018 Valencia Robin, *Ridiculous Light*
2017 Emily Van Kley, *The Cold and the Rust*
2016 Molly McCully Brown, *The Virginia State Colony for Epileptics and Feebleminded*
2015 Kimberly Grey, *The Opposite of Light*
2014 Susannah Nevison, *Teratology*
2013 Leslie Shinn, *Inside Spiders*
2012 Allison Seay, *To See the Queen*
2011 Laura Cronk, *Having Been an Accomplice*
2010 Cynthia Marie Hoffman, *Sightseer*
2009 Alexandra Teague, *Mortal Geography*
2008 Tara Bray, *Mistaken for Song*
2007 Anne Shaw, *Undertow*
2006 Alena Hairston, *The Logan Topographies*

TOWN CRIER

POEMS

Sarah Matthes

A Karen & Michael Braziller Book
PERSEA BOOKS / NEW YORK

Persea Books, Inc.
90 Broad Street
New York, New York 10004

Library of Congress Cataloging-in-Publication Data

Names: Matthes, Sarah, 1991– author.
Title: Town crier : poems / Sarah Matthes.
Description: New York : Persea Books, 2021. | "A Karen & Michael Braziller book." |
    Summary: "Kabbalistic poems that recognize wit as a ritual of mourning, winner of
    the 2020 Lexi Rudnitsky First Book Prize"—Provided by publisher.
Identifiers: LCCN 2020052502 | ISBN 9780892555277 (paperback)
Subjects: LCGFT: Poetry.
Classification: LCC PS3613.A8444 T69 2021 | DDC 811/.6—dc23
LC record available at https://lccn.loc.gov/2020052502

Book design and composition by Rita Lascaro
Typeset in Baskerville
Manufactured in the United States of America.
Printed on acid-free paper.

for Max Ritvo,
for whom nothing was trivial,
yet everything absurd

Contents

The Basics | 3

All Spruced Up | 5

The Jungle of Sick Animals | 8

The Glowing Boy | 9

Not Dying | 12

One Wish | 14

Are You Grateful for the Time We Shared | 16

Pickup Sticks | 17

613 Mitzvot | 18

Sarah? | 21

Love Poem | 22

Gyroscope | 24

The Seventeen Year Cicadas | 26

Harder All the Time to Go Back to New Jersey | 28

Subject | 31

Almost Haunted | 32

A Parent | 34

Then One Day a Whole Day Goes By | 35

Aphasia | 36

Amorphism | 38

Rodney the Mouse | 39

The Burning Bush is a Blackberry Bush | 41

Golem | 42

I Cannot Remember the Configuration of Prayer | 52

What is Left and If It's Safety | 53

"Listen, There are Demons in Your Well" | 54

Self Portrait at the End of My Life | 55

What I Would Ask You | 57

To Examine the Marks in Fishes | 58

Wet Body Hot Stone | 66

Lament for the Living | 68

Coda | 69

Golem | 70

Transitory Mitzvah | 74

Just Now with Arms Outstretched You Burst into the Room and Seize Your Old Soccer Trophy! | 76

Accidental Yahrzeit | 77

Opening | 80

Getting Out of St. Paul | 82

A Preposition to Follow "Live" | 84

Acknowledgments | 85

TOWN
CRIER

THE BASICS

I thought I understood the basics:
my body would be put through a series of trials.

I understood the surface of the water,
when broken
by a chucked stone,

would reassemble itself
around the sharp intruder—

I would not be so constant.

But even when the news of *blood* reached me,
even when the white moon sat in the white cloud of day, I believed
in a deep magnetic resolution,

the way I believe in the inevitability
of separated twins colliding at the market.

Then one day, rewarding myself for a month of consistent and
        vigorous exercise,
I took the scenic byway through a nearby mountain, and, spotting
        something
in the road ahead,
I slowed to discover

one chipmunk
facedeep
in a second, dead chipmunk,
its little mouth trembling in the soft still fur—

And I couldn't find a way around that.

I lived for years within that.

What kind of mind
is unable to recognize the difference

between a chipmunk in mourning
and a chipmunk at lunch?

ALL SPRUCED UP

"A shprikhvort iz a vorvot."
A proverb tells the truth
      —Yiddish proverb

"You can't grow corn on the ceiling"
is a Yiddish saying I particularly relate to,
not because I farm, per se

but because I do often feel the weight
of large, jeweled objects
dropped into my hands,

and tend toward hanging those kinds of things
by a string from the ceiling,
as opposed to burying them

and showing patience.
Imagine how wrong we all have it.
Had we just buried the mirrorball like G-d intended—

fuck! What sterling trees,
bearing gleaming disco fruities.
I am smote by the silver images.

"You can't outrun the moon" is another phrase
that brings me solace, because yes, thank you, I do feel
that the moon has been chasing me,

which is, I think, what they call *vanity*.
"A man should stay alive if only out of curiosity"
is good advice, though I fear most people

pay attention more to the *man*
or *alive*,
and less to *if only*.

The phrase "All spruced up" might instead be said
Vie Chavele tsu der geht, which means
"Like Eve on her way to get a divorce."

Imagine her, stepping out
of her bone cage,
ready to love the dark.

I think "All spruced up"
is the most romantic phrase
in the whole of my Yiddish phrasebook:

If only diseases stuck to clothes and thistles to the body

If only the bears were as soft as cooked carrots

If only brides were beautiful and the dead pious

If only the goose hadn't starved in those oats

If only thieves loved night for the same reason you and I do

yes you,
you, you
with the *punim*.

And what do we say of G-d?
That his ear is an oyster.
That he glitters
even in the mud—
Or was that G-ld?

No, that's what never rusts.
Never rusts—That was rain.
No, not rain—Or was that heaven?

THE JUNGLE OF SICK ANIMALS

You are there and you are the king.

This is announced by a wreath of grapes
cold and elegant against your head's bare skin.

When the grapes get hot in the jungle sun
they are rushed to a quick river
and made cool and bright again.

They go through many cycles of this.
They are very resilient grapes.

You are my most resilient grape:

Inside your body dangle hundreds of short white strings.
Inside your body lives a red-tentacled cell
that is trying to collapse you by pulling every string.

You don't have time to shrivel: you are the king,
and have things to attend to.

Look, here comes a blue sick animal
who cares too much about her hair.
Care about it for her. There goes a sturdy little bug

whose spirit is dying. Give her a grape.

And the small animals sleep in hammocks of big animals.
And the big animals gather their bodies in a warm circle.
And the rain says this is the most beautiful thing I have ever seen I am
    leaving immediately.

It feels good to have finally written a poem about your wedding.

THE GLOWING BOY

Inside your spine
a filament of light
keeps you alive.

There is an electric hum
trapped light makes and
you make it—

Your bones throw
their white shutters open
to the blood.

You gather some attention
for being
the glowing boy.

People love you, because of
or in spite of or
regardless.

Everywhere you go,
a crowd arcs in your wake,
like a sliver moon drawn

impossibly close to the sun.
So you do a little magic:
you stand, alive.

It's nobody's fault
that they've become
this thin hive—

eyes go to fire.
Your body balanced atop a slippery fulcrum.
On one side, *Laugh*—

the goonish shuffle,
the flickering skin
and odd little cap.

And on the other, *Cry*—
you take off
the cap.

How long have you lived
upon the edge of not living,
your life this great trick:

that we keep naming things
we think have disappeared
that were never even there.

Suddenly: Rain, wild and dizzy
as bees in a box, awakened by rain.
You run indoors

and hide under a sheet.
You begin
to understand

the night,
that it's
the last.

Each inhale fans the flame,
each exhale melts the lungs
to lace. The windows are full of faces.

I try: *No fear—*
Death is the final antidote
to having a body.

I try: *It's okay, it's okay,*
I'm here,
I love you.

NOT DYING

I had a book of poems I was writing you
when you were dying.

It was called *Eras*, a period of time
or a word meaning "you are,"

which you were when you were dying
and are even more now
that you're not.

Now that you're not dying anymore
I don't know what to do with those poems,

most of which I never wrote because
I didn't want you to be dying.

In place of words, death filled my mind with a navy gas.

When you stopped dying my center cooled,
and down it rained.

It hasn't gone from me.
It has found a new part of me to feed:
this is how a heart beats.

⚘

Here's a problem with this poem:

There are two ways that someone can be
not dying anymore.

You have been more than a period of time.

You are more
than what you have been.

And when you go

once more my center will cool and harden
into navy ice,

and your words will freeze in me,
and there will be no room left for other words,
and the navy will be dark.

ONE WISH

I give you one wish—
you say your wish
is to give your wish to me.

This is the central issue of our friendship:
I feel backed into a corner,
you keep insisting it's a hinge,

that we are an elbow in the universe's exasperated arm.

Just imagine, you say,
falling in love with your parallel line.
That's the saddest thing in the world.

I can think of
some other things.

What's your wish?

To be crushed to death by a meteorite
that takes the shape of my body
at the moment of impact,

replaced by a statue of my final moment
that's been hurdling toward me
since before my first.

Your voice goes glossy and garbled
on death's sharpening stone.

What's
your wish?

To build you out of glass,
a hollow golem hinged silver
down the heart.

To slide my hand
inside of yours,

and wear you
like a crystal glove.

And then
I hear you breaking
I hear you
on the other side of this
I am fairly sure
you are not

coming back

I am

A bad day
A bad day
Another
A new wish

To die
simply
from being this

ARE YOU GRATEFUL FOR THE TIME WE SHARED

Were you looking for something in nature
that *isn't* yourself, after all this time
of being human? A zipper unzips. A worried bird.
The day perfected, there is nothing left to be done.
We stare off into a pale, apassive sky.
Who is in charge here? The birds assemble
into a train track, which soon explodes
into no birds. See the dog digging in the cooling sand,
the humans digging too, drilling down a thick,
long log to be discovered later by a stranger
who will delight in the trunk bursting out of the beach,
and wonder just how deep down it must go.
The clouds are like beards of men with no faces.
The sea is the air for everything else. Oh no!
Behold! A youth has sidled up to the log, straddling it
for a photo, the whole thing an elaborate penis joke,
the picture snapped, the heart destroyed.
There is no safety save my hands over my ears,
my nose plugged up by other hands,
my eyes afraid to open to find out whose hands—

PICKUP STICKS

In my dream last night
you were great at the game.

You could surgically excise
the impossible yellow stick,

sealing the delicate pile still
with your gel-like breath,

which poured over the sticks
and onto my fingers

in a wet, round cloud.
Great, okay, I get it—

what the dead do is float.
So maybe the afterlife

is just another planet.

Maybe it's close.

Maybe I can see it from here.

And then I looked up,

and the day was so grey and comprehendible—

613 MITZVOT

I've been to this park before.
I'm starting to accrue on this place,
my presence a little bump of spackle
where a better picture hung.

A Tinder message comes in:
Wait is that you in the park right now?

It feels
so good
to be recognized.

I shut that down fast though
by talking too much about the 613 mitzvot,
and the categories into which I am sorting them:
confusing; amazing; terrifying; important.

The guy was like,

k.

You know how it feels when you're on to something?

The sea closing up behind Moses and Aaron,
inventing the zipper, eventually—
A cloud exhaling slow over the sun,
shapes moving on the grass—

I lived my whole life thinking I mostly got it:
There would be hardships, sure,
but there would also be cross-stitches,
paring knives, parables—ways.

And then the arrival of blood, and its usual
readjustments. Then the condemnation of love,
first G-d of my life, followed shortly by
Trees, Steam, Travel by Wind—

And then these 613 small new g-ds:

Not to eat things that swarm in the water.
Not to muzzle a beast, while it is working in produce
which it can taste and enjoy.
Not to leave something that might cause hurt.
Not to seek the dead.

Anyway, 6 + 1 + 3 = 10
which is one of my favorite numbers,
while 6 − 1 − 3 = 2
which is, you guessed it, my other favorite number.

Is this a numerological mysticism? Is this
the transformation of 10 to ten, of 12 to a dozen,
of 2, inevitably, to parting?

Somewhere in the number line, there exists
my perfect balanced name.

Imagine it: se.lf,
a quantity of language,
more than I or me.

Sara.h with her dangling breath,
her name the red leave-a-penny dish
into which we drop a copper "h,"
suddenly with something to give.

But some days the decimal shifts underneath me.
Some days I am floating
with my ears under the wa.ter—

lo.ve, rounded up,
becomes the way I feel without it: low—

go.d wakes me up
and all that's left by night is go—

SARAH?

It wasn't my name that was said. It was just the word "sincerity,"
but I inserted myself into the conversation anyway,
and I had a lot to say.

Walking home, I remember my favorite ever explanation
of magic. It's about learning the true name of the sea,
and then you have it.

I designed a line of hats, dark and ballooning. My investors
shook their heads. "Who is your girl?" they asked me.
"Do you really think she would wear all of those sorrows?"

An important part of me is the smell of birds.
Each wing perfumed by the safety of trees. Each perfume
swung by seraphim, the wrong godly bringer of the bad bird.

One day you said "serenade me." Sure.
That's when I take your hand around my wrist
and you feel the wild moths.

Just a quick memory here: making Jell-O when mom and dad
were out, spilling the unset mess all over our feet
because we had forgotten the saran wrap. Washing each other's feet.

Can I borrow your hands? I need to quickly mummify
this thing right here between us. Bring me a triceratops.
I will die in a glow. Samsara, samsara—I will never die.

LOVE POEM

Some days I wake up
and it is terrifying.

A dream of you is only "good"
while it's happening—then

it's just pissing with an open door, missing
the deeply imagined thing,

wondering how will I ever know
if I really came in my sleep?

You're so enthusiastic.
Your midwife roommate

has used your dehydrator
for her clients' many placentas.

The machine is clean and damp on the drying rack,
you could proceed, you could make your beef jerky,

but instead you must call and let me know
about the dehydrated placenta.

This is one way that you tell me
that you love me.

Another is when you leave a package in your freezer
clearly marked:

"SNAKE: DO NOT EAT."
I appreciate that.

But sometimes affection
is a salve we rub over affliction,

like the way you take the unknown calls
that come into my phone from 609 area codes,

and never disparage me for assuming they carry news
of fresh death.

The way, once, you listened
as I practiced a eulogy between bites of pickled radish.

Do you remember that dim afternoon?
Curled like quotation marks on the bed.

A mouth opened
between us.

Holding each other, kissing casually,
you started to squirm,

rolling your forehead
over and over my chest.

Do you remember how you said it,
the very first time you said it?

You answered "I love you."
I had asked "What's wrong?"

GYROSCOPE

You are learning everything about how to get around in this world
if your phone is dead, and your sextant has been crushed

by your enemies. *One old sailors' trick,* you tell me,
was to stand nude on the ship's deck

and note which way the testicles swayed
to determine the swell of the sea.

This was difficult to corroborate on the internet.
It was, however, an effective seduction.

You can tell north from the stars and south from the moon—
you know the winds from the birds and the weather from the winds,

the hours from your palms stacked up on the horizon, measuring the sky
like a horse's wide grey side. But for someone so devoted

to knowing where we're going,
you never can remember where we've been—

It was a concert, summer, there was a long hill and a big green crowd,
were you there? Yes, I got separated from the group

and you found me panicking by the porta-potties,
like a child "staying put."

There was a cardinal, so early in its season, lifting
against the wind's northern shift, when was that?

That was when I wrote you a letter.
It was in the letter I wrote.

Of all the senses hiding in the helices of other senses,
nearness is the one.

Sometimes, I close my eyes.
Then I know where I am.

THE SEVENTEEN YEAR CICADAS

We dared each other to eat them

A dollar for a hollow husk
Two for the living ones

Some bodies are warmer than others
Some sweat is so sweet

Wading ankle-deep
The dead crisp foliage of wings

I got to touch you
Brushing one off your neck
Pinky skimming the hot cotton of your summer shirt

The flinch of your body
The tightening skin

You lit up
Either your chest beating forward or
Your shoulders cringing away

That distinction making all the difference in my world

And I was unsure
And I was ashamed

And then I went around touching everyone for years
Blaming cicadas

Can you imagine it
Standing young and shoeless in a purple dusk

The field so empty
The trees so still
Wondering *where did all their bodies go*

They were just here
Right here

The sound still humming in your memory like a grooved tinnitus

Can you discern it

The difference between what you loved
And what was there

The trees so empty
The field so still

Like the living room the morning after a party
When you wander downstairs to find everyone

Has rolled away their sleeping bags
And gone to the lake without you

HARDER ALL THE TIME
TO GO BACK TO NEW JERSEY

My old friend makes me sit in the car forever
when we get to the bar
to feel the way the engine "purrs" or something

and having never engaged in such a predictable show
of homo-vehicular sensuality,

I sink into the seat and paw
his jacket for a lighter.

Hold my cold hands up
to my cold face.
Try to discern what is colder.

Inside eventually,
there is all-you-can-eat crab
someone is eating

in quantities
so normal
it breaks my heart.

Put on something sad, friends,
let's clear this place out.

I remember when:
low brown ceiling.
Mural of women in stiff bonnets.

Listen, I *know* how to pour a beer
so that it doesn't foam over,
I just didn't.

Across from me is a girl
who greatly hurt a friend of mine who,
in two weeks' time, will greatly hurt me,

so, you know, pick your battles.

The one I pick with her tonight
is about our order of potato skins.

I want to know what they do with the potatoes.

"They skin them" she says.

I hate her so much
I want to kiss her,
long and surprising,
with the loudest "mwah."

Everyone is outside smoking.

I'll go when they come back.

Behold: an orphaned potato skin.
I set it down like a boat
in the closed sea of my glass,

watch the salt blast the beer
into a fizzing, electric kiss, and go back—

Pop rocks. Purple sky. Under the bradford pear trees.

There's a special darkness cast around
a single light left on at home.

Sometimes I think if I had known
they were just joking about eating the roach.

If I hadn't pretended my voice was lost
a day after it had come back.

If only I had known that the ones I would love
were the ones that would never leave

and that the staying would make them
so unlovable.

SUBJECT

I wanted to make a museum
comprised entirely of relics
from my most beloved friends.

I wanted to put strange fuzz
under glass and keep it
forever strange and fuzzy.

During the period of my life
when I daily scooped lint
from my love's bellybutton

and kept it safe in a plastic bag,
you alone I told. You understood
my foresight:

the deep spice of the invasion,
and its promise of
good kindling for fire.

Your plinth would be empty,
glass trapping a piece of air
dark and full of gravity.

ALMOST HAUNTED

Alone in bed, I scroll through videos
dull enough to bring sleep. Readjusting my headphones,
I hear a voice in my left ear. *Sarah?*
I whack the earbud away, flipping the computer on its back
so the blue light glows into the shadows
of the empty room. Everything is growing,
even the complicated cells of my eyes,
the simple ones that make a ring of me.

Fear is made one part of stillness.
Have you ever nearly fallen off
of something very tall, onto something very hard?
And were you charged electric
by the great pause, the skillful eye of terror
locking you out
of your body's house?

I slowly reinsert the earbud
into my head.

Hello? I say.
Are you there?

The quietness resumes into a black
plastic ribbon
taping over my visions.

But we forget these things.

So in the morning when the kitchen light
is flickering like a metronome

I don't think
before I unscrew the hissing bulb

and place you delicately in the blue recycling bin.

A PARENT

There is only one part of you left
that is not underground—

your sample,
shivering in a freezer,

your half-children crying out
their one shared name.

Some bad thing in me
waits until the bird is full

of worm for its babies. Then
the bad thing eats the bird.

THEN ONE DAY A WHOLE DAY GOES BY

Then one day a whole day goes by.
You're not in the tree. You're not even
in the bird.

Someone keeps erasing your nose.
Someone keeps painting huge white
swatches behind your glasses, which
keep falling off your face because
no nose.

In the morning in the dark in the cold outside
I raised my finger to touch what I believed

to be the first frost of the season,
navy ice lacing across
the rear windshield of my car,

but when I stroked the glass
it crumbled.

APHASIA

The barista I knew when I was young
says *Come, sit with me*,
and tells me how he doesn't believe
in reality anymore.

This chair, these teeth
could be anything
that isn't a chair,
or teeth.

I'm not interested in his latest endeavor,
a drawing he shows me, naming it "Shame."
A sketch of a man: such large hands over
what kind of face.

I have to go, or I say so, and sit on the street
that erupts twice a year:
once with white pear blossoms, once
in bare wired branches—vibrations in the sky.

At home my father watches the television
muted, saying *Who is this*, and *What*
are these fellows doing, and every few minutes
he hears a sound

that might be the ice box
spawning, and on double canes
he walks to the front door,
like a paper puppet shaking in the light.

I am going to stay on this bench a very long time,
watching autumn's fingers paint salted lines

around the spaces where the leaves have pressed
their damp brown bodies to the ground,

and I will try to find a way to carve the space around my body
into quiet, or lift a spindle
from my tongue to tighten these sounds
into simply something else.

When I finally go home, I am going
to ask my father how his day was, and he'll say *The egg*
is on top of the egg but he won't mean an egg
and he won't mean an egg.

AMORPHISM

There must be a song that birds use
to describe a form of clairvoyance
based on the motions
of our human commutes,

or the family tree
of a tree
drawn in the shape of man
recycling himself underground.

There must be an angler fish
so deep in the squeeze
of the ocean's core
alighting its ancient leather face
like a nightmare in the nightlight in the night.

I love the Komodo dragon sleeping in the zoo,
his poison tongue locked in his jaw,
his breath bluing the glass for a moment like smoke.

I love the Loch Ness Monster
because I know she is a stick.

RODNEY THE MOUSE

Rodney, my angel,
my midnight hunter, my regular
family man,

tonight no one is watching
the moon lay its satins across the tile.
No one hears the cold
kick the pane glass. No one cleaned
the egg pan either.

This is your world, Rodney.

I've been noticing recently that my shits
have been looking more like your shits. Rodney,
is this because we're on the same diet?

Are we made of the same tubes,
the same gauze that keeps it together?

Little lord, sweet
patriarch,

I'm going to kill your family. One by one,
in the snap trap in my closet. I'll stiffen
each tail to wire, a hard little lightning strike.

Your wife is a hedonist, she lives in my oven.

Rodney, I've been having this recurring
dream, it always starts the same way:
palms full of tiny mouse ears.

I pinch another off my eyeball like a contact lens.

I place the ears carefully on the pads of my fingertips
and hold them out in clemency.
Then one by one I eat them.

This is usually
something done at a party,
sexily, with olives.

THE BURNING BUSH IS A BLACKBERRY BUSH

I wrote the poem. And then I rewrote it, and made it worse.
I thought time would heal it. Time passed. I did research: Exodus,
midrash, my mother. I rewrote the poem. I ate fistfuls of soft berries. Navy
lips. Purple lips. Juice bursting out of black balloons. I made it worse.
The poem knocked around my mind like unlabeled preserves darkening
     in the fridge.
Outside the page: tableaus of simple beauty.
Three different trees in one line of sight—plum, pear, palm.
Inside: A hand runs under a faucet, the soap stinging invisible cuts to life.

Have you seen a blackberry bush at the exact moment of its blushing,
when its tight little spheres bleed the green seeds bloody—
have you walked by shoeless on the way to the lake,
the sun lifting the hairs on your cheek,
no matter where you turn, something you love coming after you,
the bush burning in the stripped light,
unripe, alive, surviving—

GOLEM

Adam sat sucking onion grass.
Dragged his teeth across the stones where he pounded round berries.
Licked circles in the dirt. Tongued one by one his fingers,
matting the clay of his body into a shape,

and when his belly ached and he called out, his hunger
was mistaken for loneliness.

The red rib torn out like a sapling uprooted.

But joyous bend! He sat self-fellating on the riverbank.

And he sat like that for days.

His body took the shape of the letter *tet*,
letter of concealed good,
letter of the fetus.

❉

In Prague golem protected us from—reports vary.
Some bad breath curled through the square. Wood doors
closed securely in their brick cradles. Inside our little rooms,
we kept our hands held tight.

We always made sure to have an alibi of hands.

Outside: a cart drags along the cobbled street. The butcher
carries his meats from the slaughterhouse,
back through the Jewish ghetto.

At his shop, he hauls a heavy hog from the pile
that flickers with black flies. He does not notice
the seam in the pig's stomach,
the pink stitches that lace up
the waxen skin. He does not know
about the child.

Tomorrow, he will notice the *tallis* dangling from the pig's mouth, stained
an unfamiliar dark red.

He will feel proud, for a moment, having identified
the interloping
human blood.

☸

Humans are made of bones. Imagine a cave, sealed
by immovable stones. If blood runs down the walls,
would you say that cave is bleeding? Now
look at me.

Who comes to break me open? Golem means *unfinished mass*. Golem
means *embryo*.

Once there was a poet, eleventh century Spain,
face bubbling with leprosy, a mind so wide with language
that his skin could not contain him.

That summer it stormed perhaps,
or heat lightning struck at a distance
with no warning and no thunder.
The door blew off its hinges five times before
autumn cooled all things into their place.

At night he chopped
the wood to sticks
with a dull, heavy hatchet:
Fingers, legs, a number of ribs.
He twisted hinges
into a bright spine—gathered whittled wisps
into a tight pubic curl.
He made a wooden girl.
By winter, golem made him warm.

❧

Golem stands aproned in the kitchen
shucking scales off a slim mackerel.

Oil spits in the iron over a fire.

With a silver spoon she gouges the eyes
neatly out of the fish's surprised face,
and pops them into her own rough sockets.

The sound of a creaking door as
something in her
smiles.

※

Golem gives the poet baths,
depleting a sponge
over his shoulders.

Her hands become swollen and water-logged.
They begin to rot. As he soaks, she readies
the bedroom. She cracks
a fresh sheet into the air.

When he comes to her he holds a can of oil,
bids her sit on the edge of the bed.

In rivulets he wets her hinges—gentle, deliberate.
He writes letters on her metal. A verse
runs liquid down her knees.

When he fucks her, she tears his body apart. His skin raked red
by her splinters. Blood on the sheets his blood. Tomorrow
she will wash them.

Tonight, she lets the termites in her mouth
soothe her into a sleep. They lozenge her throat.
They feel her larynx tremor and hum,
and set to work building her a tongue.

❀

The neighbors see a tree moving through the forest.

Three men come to the house by torchlight.

She holds a shaking ladle toward the door.

The poet writes
in the tepid night
by a wailing fire.

❀

Sometimes women like me are called golems, too.
Not human until another human beats inside us.

You don't have to marry me. You already
did. That bleak afternoon I lost
the tampon string, couldn't search it out
where it had shriveled deep inside me.

Like a surgeon you washed and gloved your hands
and carefully rolled a finger through the unseen cave of my body.

You emerged, rouged and exhilarated.
There's nothing inside you.
I went to the doctor for a second opinion.

Did you write your name inside me that day? *Yod Shin Yod*:
—a divine point—
—a sharp press—
—a divine point—

What is bleeding is it
just blood, moving—
am I doing it now as I
come to you—

I CANNOT REMEMBER THE
CONFIGURATION OF PRAYER

Something goes inside of something else,

something speaks and touches or
is touched by what is spoken

and is any of it me?

WHAT IS LEFT AND IF IT'S SAFETY

I have a plan a vision—
Did I already tell you this?
How many children do I want?
Negative three.

When traveling I break
all my rules.

I eat tube meats
and drink coffee
after alcohol
and then again.

Listen: I've slept with men
for protection
in unfamiliar cities.

It's the best way,
I promise.
You just have to keep saying:
I chose this—I chose this—I chose this.

Sometimes, if you say it out loud,
it'll be so off-putting
that the man will become uncomfortable

and then you won't have to choose.

"LISTEN, THERE ARE DEMONS IN YOUR WELL"

I am bound in a complicated braid.
Voices, they wind through
my many ducts—
ventricles and veins, round vowels.

An O is a heavy roll
of paper towels
impossibly knocked over
in a midnight kitchen.

In bed I wonder why the cat is shaking
until I realize I'm shaking
and that I'm shaking the cat.

Listen, I know that there are demons in my well.
I can feel their fists pounding
my empty cavities.

The stories tell me to extricate the demons,
I need only throw my nagging wife
down the well, and she will drive them away.

Being my own wife, I chuck myself
into the dark.

I fall for a very long time.

Turning myself inside out
is much less terrifying than expected:

It's really good to see you—

SELF PORTRAIT AT THE END OF MY LIFE

I do remember beauty:

A blue pool in the pine barrens,
the fermata of a summer afternoon,
tangles of hair on a soft stomach,
my lips combing through them;

Working quick and hard on a fire
in the black backyard, knowing soon
I'd see those bright lit faces bursting
through the screen door
saying *there you are*;

And then being alone:
howling on the mountain
until my spirit expands, pans out
and sees my body disappear
below the tree-line;

Or the vast expansive solitude
of being a child in the backseat of the car
at the end of a long trip home, the hum
of adult voices, my head cradled in the sling of the seatbelt,
the dark and permeable glass,
the sky spilling in—

Still, I wanted the next thing.

To collapse the paper dolls of my life
back into the flank of an aspen.

To hear the insides,
like floating with your ears below the water.

I suppose that's what I'm getting now,
though I always pictured it differently.

I thought I'd be on my back.

WHAT I WOULD ASK YOU

Friend,
when the end comes,
who takes the blood from us?

The earth or the air—

Which did you choose—

TO EXAMINE THE MARKS IN FISHES

> *But we were not born to survive*
> *Only to live*
>   W. S. Merwin

I.

On the bank of the river.
The forest burning behind me.

The red bird peels out of air
with the resistance of an underripe banana.

Tight in my left fist,
a wet and seizing fish.

If I hold the fish much longer out of water it will die.
The word that lives below "suffocation"
like weasels under the damp wood house
lifts its head.

II.

If I set the fish in the river,
the bird
will fish it out.

Of all the things our human tongues have done,
"fishing" is perhaps the greatest violence:

Making a name into a word
that means to kill the name.

III.

I think I am supposed to save us all—

some sequence of holding and letting go,
some faith,
like spinning past the number
on the combination lock,
knowing it will return.

The word that lives above "suffocation"
like rats in the attic
sucks its pulsing finger.

IV.

The longer I wait
the more we are becoming
meat.

It's a warm, runny feeling—
Finding out which parts of me
soften, which crisp.

What part was blue all along
like a lobster's cooled secret.

V.

There was a moment in this poem
when I walked into and out of a riddle
with the swift indifference
of a swinging silver pendulum,

when I could have slipped my tongue
like a wet key
into the air's warm door.

Do you remember the bird
and how she sort of came out of a banana?
I felt weird about that.

But at the moment I saw it,
clear and bright and physical
as a papier-mâché mobile of the sun
and its adorers.

There is a word
living inside the word "breathing,"
like a caged bird covered by thick muslin.

It's smaller than the shape
my mouth makes to say it—

quicker,
like pointing to the night sky,
and saying only "never mind,
you missed it."

VI.

The fire rolling over the ridge line,
drawing its yellow hands the wrong way across
the thick green velvet trees.

The fish still living,
in my hand, sizzling.

The bird suddenly on the opposite bank
of the river, wings thrown open
in dismay and squawking like a parent
watching its child loop daisies in the outfield.

VII.

Again and again misremembering
the solutions to those riddles:

A crisp cabbage knocked about
in the bottom of a damp, wood boat,
the boat rowed across the river
by a drooling fox.

A woman
naked in the woods
lighting a single match.

A woman screaming at one of two doors.

VIII.

What if the rules applied?
And I knew the answer
because the riddle was my design.

And fishing was a jubilee
that slapped bright shapes into the river.

What hunger could we feed
with our own deep
red meat? How do I find my magnet
without my magnet to pull me there?

Can I blank the paper?
Can I push it, uncut and sopping,
back into its pulp?

I press my fingers through my eyes
and the riddle is solved, the river
resolved, the bird zipping itself
into the banana, the fire gasped back
into the mind's sagging lung—

Can I save this place? O
let me save this place.
O let me bring myself
to leave it behind—

WET BODY HOT STONE

In everything, I see only myself—
no need to paint irises on stones.

Dark fish gasp across rapids,
and my lungs and stomach gather

in a tight bouquet to spice the blood.
I cut my finger—the skin grows back

strong and smooth—
a new bright brick in my barricade.

Then comes the night
and there are no stilting tree tops

to make into my fingers, no nape of neck
pressed into this ditch of clay.

Night eats the liver
out of the river's stunned pools.

There must be more left than my mind.

Universe, please—
send me the shade of someone I love.

The old woman made of nightmare
who sits on my chest—even she
has her bad dreams.

My life has been the wet imprint
of someone else's body

as they rise from a wide, hot stone
and take to the river to rinse again.

When I die free me from parallel—

Let me feed every tree—

LAMENT FOR THE LIVING

We feel them walking over us in their intolerable shoes,
knocking down our stone doors. And what
would they have us do—come outside?
We will not afternoon among the pigeons,
who loiter like blanched old men in a sauna,
moaning "arrgargahhh" but meaning to say
"shut the door" but meaning "let this day
end me." Their dicks lolling across their thighs,
gummy and white as gefilte fish.
                              Overwrought? Yes.
But this is just one tunnel through the story,
and it is not the one that leads to some outside
that is sweet and green. What if we had known
we were in the last five years of our lives?
What a relief! To look around and say
how fine it is, to awaken in the cracked sun,
to knock back a berry into our mouths
like a large and living pill! To have two
and a half years to eat before our time is reset
into a new measure of halfness. And it goes.
For decades we split ourselves across the longing
of an asymptote, until one day we reach down to wipe
and we're putting our hand
                              through a ghost.
And then it becomes intolerable. Like fruit salad—
a grape disguised in the juices of a cantaloupe.
We leave behind a dotted line, and all these *people!*
They follow it like a map to heaven,
when all we meant was "cut here."

CODA

When a child is conceived, the bones are said to come from the man,
the skin and muscles from the woman,
the senses from G-d.

This sounds wrong to me:

Remember when my wrist bone broke through, slashing
the blue blood strings

and my glossy eyes darkening,

the slip of body and mind into one cleaved ridge
(the sharp surprising seam on a soft rubber thing in a baby's mouth)—

I felt a lot of things in that final moment.
Let's begin with the love I bore for myself:

GOLEM

I could build a golem out of all the hair
I have ever removed from my body. The neck
young locks. Round pubic bursts of eyes.
I could dye its cheeks
with indigo and lemon.

She waits outside the cafe,
licking ankles like a dog.

At dinner she stands behind me and makes a red thread necklace
as strands falls in my eggplant.

I awaken in a whelp of pain.
Golem pulling out my long eyebrow hairs
with her teeth, adding them
to the contour of her elbow.

I attempt an adult conversation about it.
I use non-accusatory language. I offer her
the harvestings of my brush, which she pushes
into a clavicle bone, and begins to cry.

Golem cries sweat. Anyone else would think she were sweating,
if not for the sound:

From her wiry gape of mouth, an entire orchestra breaks
one string each.

In the morning I find her sleeping in the sectioned sunlight on the tile. Breath like a sharpening stone.

She has made herself a tail.

Each time I undress we play
the mirror game.

We stand naked
across from each other

and practice
different feelings.

She makes a shape
with her body,

and I feel for her
the shape she shows.

But the game always ends
so badly. I know

when she performs
"sadness"

she is thinking only
of us, and I am thinking instead

of the oldest people
in the world,

trying
to walk up some stairs.

She wouldn't understand this.
My poor phantom thing.

Even the greatest sculptures lack
stomach and lung—human hollowness.

Wherever she is now,
I want her to know this:

that she was conceived when I pulled
a single hair from my mouth
during an extended fellatio:

like all those glad little girls,
she was made in an act of love.

TRANSITORY MITZVAH

In the subway car, a mystery of proximity: a yawn
passing from mouth to mouth,
across a line of seated strangers,
in perfect order. I watched it moving

like a secret through a row of children,
washing toward me as each person opened
their lips to swallow it up
and then, in unbroken revolution,
give it away.

I thought this must be G-d: air
moving through human bodies
like a soft needle picking up stitches along pale cloth.

And I felt my neighbor expand
in her crest of breath, hand
floating to her mouth
like wood rising in water,

and I prepared myself for the gift—

But the yawn turned across the aisle.
I saw it grow inside a child and then drift
into his mother, as it passed again

and again away from me.

What would you unsee
so you could be inside of it?

Could it ever be enough just to say:
it happened, nothing opened
or closed around me, air moved
and was wind, air moved and was
breath, air moved and was death,
my life, it did not change—

JUST NOW WITH ARMS OUTSTRETCHED YOU BURST INTO THE ROOM AND SEIZE YOUR OLD SOCCER TROPHY!

—only to remove the box of nails
tucked as a plinth beneath it.

You select one
delicately
and return to your hammer.

But O, the moment
as it had been,

the electric silhouette
of someone who,
working in the yard, is gripped
with a sudden and perfect need
to hold their plastic trophy.

It's always the same:

Time moves through things
I love and
it moves them and
is breaking.

ACCIDENTAL YAHRZEIT

It is still early December, it is the beginning
of the season of the death days
of so many I loved,

and the birthdays
of those other dead
who died in different seasons,

and the days are full
of meaningful oak leaves,
specific soups, a little sudden

crying by
the sheer
blue curtains—

you know when the sun catches
a whole universe
of hanging dust?

A bit of light better lit
by all the light
that surrounds it?

Under a white
draped cloth,
what you had made me:

a menorah.
Black and steel. Slim welds.
Opening fingers.

And the candles were too large
for their metal wells,
so we whittled them thinner with paring knives.

And you don't know
that the holiday ended days ago—
And I'm not going tell you.

Nine white lights
open their eyes to a night
they've never seen, and the record player

spins a slipping voice through the room,
the heat is on, the couch is green,
the dark days of my longing

approach, they turn up my street,
they fill my yard with omens:
a sneaker tread, a grey fox

and a red, both
together,
a sapling seizing out of the ground

like an arm. But inside,
your arm is around me—
outside there is loss but inside

there is a deep
and abiding
remainder,

tomorrow there is all that
but look,
look at now,

this: my sorrow
suspended in your steel,
my light lit up in your love.

OPENING

Before those other befores
there was a static. A vibrating mind,
jeans slipped on the body
fresh and hot from the dryer, full
of surprising thorns.

Then a long, clean pour

and that was you—

water cohering its round, bouncing molecules
into a ribbon.

I stunned into a pool.

Someone grabs my hand in the parking lot,
then apologizes. They thought I was someone else.

How close I was to being the one they were longing for,
my cheek like the atmosphere of the cheek they crave.

How sad, to mistake the one you love
for someone else—
for the one you love to be
mistakable.

I keep that touch
like the memory of other lovers
and other others
I had before you.

All those befores, all those bodies—
I tell you they did not know me either.
They too thought I was someone else.

And to be mistaken—it takes from me.

I have been folded
and I have been ripped

but for you I open
as a paper star—

GETTING OUT OF ST. PAUL

Hiding
in the tall grass
on the north

side of the tracks,
you're trying
to pull the burrs

out of my hair.
It's night.
My pack bolsters below my knees.

I crane my ear to the east
listening for the hum
of shifting steel.

Light another,
smoke silent
and slow. Calm

myself
by thinking
things I know:

that there are
other people
in the world,

that the heart
is a fingerless
glove.

I don't want new
thoughts, don't want
to look beyond

the next train.
A switchman rolls by
in an ancient caboose, laughing

at his radio. He knows
that there are other people
in the world.

Slip
your glove
around me.

From across the tracks
I imagine a bull
is watching us.

He sees two lost fireflies
alighting
and darkening, rising

and falling,
and, at the arrival
of a sweet,

low sound
in the distance,
suddenly going out.

A PREPOSITION TO FOLLOW "LIVE"

Here I am
in someone else's bad dream.

Metal spheres roll through the grass,
grow larger, pull iron from the rock
and from the blood.

The wind takes what from me?
No matter. That was never mine.

There is burning.

When I awake the field is made of faces.
Can you remember anything?

Yes,

though how to put it.
What do you want to know?

The facts?—The feelings?
That I was there?—That I was crying?
I held a vase. I held an urn.
I was a flower.
I was what burned.

If I don't survive it, please
remember the
right things about me:

The time I was caught singing
among the violins.

Perhaps I lost my bow,
thought no one would notice the difference.

Perhaps
my voice came back
and so I used my voice.

Acknowledgments

Thanks to the following journals, in which these poems initially appeared:

"Transitory Mitzvah" in *BOAAT*

"Amorphism" in *jubilat*

"The Glowing Boy" in *The Journal*

"Lament for the Living" in *Pleiades*

"The Jungle of Sick Animals" in *The Iowa Review*

"Getting Out of St. Paul" in *Borderlands: Texas Poetry Review*

"613 Mitzvot" at *poets.org*

"Wet Body Hot Stone" and "The Seventeen Year Cicadas" at *Tor House Online*

"A Preposition to Follow 'Live'" in *Yalobusha Review*

"All Spruced Up" in *The Iowa Review Online*

"Rodney the Mouse" at *His Majesty the Baby Online Zine*

"Aphasia" in *The Bad Version*

My gratitude to my teachers: Louise Glück, Lisa Olstein, Jane Miller, Natalie Diaz, Naomi Shihab Nye, Bev Gallagher, and Judy Michaels. To everyone at the Michener Center and Persea Books.

My gratitude to my friends: Chessy Normile, Ally Glass-Katz, Leah Yacknin-Dawson, Thom May, Brielle Greek, Kelsey Burns, Willa Fitzgerald, Lucia Bonsack, Emmalee Carr, Camille Fenton, Titus Levy, Hannah McDermott, Christian Rees, and Victoria Ritvo.

My gratitude to my family: Elisa, Dick, Erich, Jackie, Henry, Kent, Barbara, and Jesse.

And of course to Max, who was and is my friend, family, and teacher.

A special thanks to my friend Ava Kofman, whose perfect description of Max serves as the dedication of this book